I am so grateful
that these words
bring a bridge
to a poetic
friendship
♡ Margo

To Day

poems & poetics
margo fuchs-knill

To Day
Margo Fuchs-Knill

ISBN 0-9685330-4-3

Published by

E·G·S
PRESS
128 Danforth Avenue, #119
Toronto, Ontario • M4K 1N1 • Canada
www.egspress.com • info@egspress.com
tel 416 778 1279

OTHER TITLES AVAILABLE FROM EGS PRESS:

Tending the Fire: Studies in Art, Therapy and Creativity
(Ellen Levine)

Minstrels of Soul: Intermodal Expressive Therapy
(Paolo Knill et al)

Crossing Boundaries: Explorations in Therapy and the Arts—
A Festschrift for Paolo Knill
(Stephen K. Levine, Editor)

POIESIS: A Journal of the Arts & Communication
Published annually

Printed in Canada

DAY POEMS

FOR THE LIVING IS TACITURN

Margo Fuchs-Knill's voice is particular: a Swiss writer immersed in the stew of American English. She knows what it means to be abandoned at school age by the mother-tongue she moves in, to be hungry for something she has not yet tasted but remembers from some other displacement. She possesses the serious playfulness of a poet, seeing and fielding words within worlds, uncovering odd nests of order in the inescapable present mess, and leaping deftly back and forth, into and out of the realms of the body's imagination.

What's a life worth living?
Honey on longing's sidewalk
Add a zest of pepper
knowing that even bitter almonds
turn into the sweetest marzipan

Margo Fuchs-Knill's second collection *To Day* moves brightly with an original Swiss-American voice and a distinctive American-Swiss pitch. The book is soaked with a sense of things moving in the calm and urgency of her experience. Most of the poems contain a running discourse on the nature of time and how we choose to live in it, through it, and despite it. Her words are flavored with the taste of savored moments, steeped in the scent of remembrance, and simmered slowly in the juices of the wild word quest, taking her listeners into familiar sanctuaries and far-flung structures at the edge of future sentences.

> *yet today one became entangled*
> *in my aged long maiden braid*
> *and the breeze from a green kiss was enough*
> *to let the not-yet through*

Margo Fuchs-Knill's essays in *To Day* on language and poetics are ready with humor and humanity, political, philosophical and psychological insights and everyday trials; she often invites her listeners to laugh quietly at the absurd human imprint at the core of language and life. At the moment that she experiences the transitory arc of longing, she is enthralled by the fully sustained moment, mischievously transformed into wordsnacks she nibbles on the run.

If forgiveness has a color, it must be the color of the dove of peace.

Elizabeth Gordon McKim
Editor and Poet
Author of *The Red Thread*

A work of art needs to be conceived—
two things coming together in the conjuring act:
the sperm of the aggressive will of going to try it and
the egg of receptiveness for the unknown.
Sometimes this union is fertile and other times not.

Margo Fuchs-Knill

Part I

AND NEVERTHELESS

I'

Bent
lightening
Remembrance cries
out—
your place, no place, one place—remains
vacant

Behold
the all-powerful, who am I
in the midst of the vast worlding?
Upright our way
only a straw in the purgatory of time
its heat kindles a next after
and this is us and you and I.

Now I say
an Amen to death
and to the mossy life
and to the vanishing kiss
and to the diminishing snail-pace
and to the last good-bye
and to this-time and now-time

empty of all beckoning.[2]

This day, like every day
stretched between ever and ever
challenges the invincible love—
an upheaval into the bottomless You.

Life's tucked creatures
crawl out from all fissures
and snuggle leisurely on my bosom

yet today one became entangled
in my aged long maiden braid
and the breeze from a green kiss was enough
to let the not-yet through.[3]

What's a life worth living?
Honey on longing's sidewalk
Add a zest of pepper
knowing that even bitter almonds
turn into the sweetest marzipan.

Again and again, call for the lost voice
again and again, dig into the silenced hole
again and again, a tear of embrace.

Hold
hold it through
hold with it
give it a hold

without holding on
to what holds It
together.

II
_____

With every good-bye
longing becomes the caretaker of remembrance
With every good-bye
emptiness shakes the future into presence.

With separation we grow.
In separation we get slow.
Through separation we fall into our own arms.

Poetry connects the
never-ending selfish story of daily life
to a pearl row
moving the horizon to a further place

to learn the alphabet from another view.

Imagine all words
would become bluish butterflies—
lofty gliding stillness.

Breaking in
breaking down
breaking up
for the
breaking through
of the steady stream
of life's undoing.

The imaginative faculty
takes its stance
for the blues of the twilight
where sky and earth
mingle.

The imaginative faculty
animates a
breathing space
for the nomadic mystery.

SPEAK TO US

And so it happened that we demanded:
Speak to us,
Son of the rounding sky,
Daughter of the turning earth.

The first one who spoke up was Impatience:
I want us to act, to make peace happen now.
It is not my nature to wait
with bent head and half-closed eyes,
dizzying the upright thinking.
I am a runner, a climber.

And so it happened that we demanded:
Speak to us,
Inspirit, thin breathing space,
upholder of the native word ex nihilo.

The second one who spoke up was Quietude:
I have endured all the weathers
of human lives at neighboring distance:
close-ups, fading into dust:
seasons of being, breezes of uproar.
It is not my nature to make the rocks fall apart.
I am the vanishing turning point
in the crack of difference,
the place to kneel
and fold your hands.

Please let me, let us
raise our arms
to praise, to praise
you, mountain, peaking
into the lit blue sky.

Mountain, urge me, urge us
to praise
the people
that love and suffer and care
the people
that did it before
to tune me, to tune us
that peace can reside.

Mountain, urge me, urge us
to praise, to praise
us climbers, us divers as far as
the word that cannot be spoken
the word that will not kill the living
the word that will not haunt the dead
the word that needs to be lived
the word that wants to be invented
by you, by me,
as us.

The word that breaks the talking
the word that spreads like fire in the wind.

Praise me, now

a/bé
a/whé
a/mà
a/schà
ma/hum
ma/hum.

I am the one that silently lifts your wandering sight.
Praise me, now
bare-rocked I am in the penetrating light

a/bé
a/whé
a/mà
a/schà
ma/hum
ma/hum.

I house your searching sight that cannot travel into me.
Praise me, now
tree green, roofless top, running waters

a/bé
a/whé
a/mà
a/schà
ma/hum
ma/hum.

I am your deep sleeper
Praise me, now

a/bé
a/whé
a/mà
a/schà
ma/hum
ma/hum.

A RESPONSE TO NELSON MANDELA

What is our deepest fear?
No longer is our deepest fear to be inadequate.
We are adequate enough to be inadequate.

What is our deepest joy?
No longer is our deepest joy to be lasting.
We have grown enough through centuries
to be short-lived.

We are longing's child of given love.
We shall taste the fruits before they rot.
We shall put our feet on this muddy earth
where bones and stones reside
to set our tiny footprints
for a future ground beyond our reach

to set our longings free.

STEPPING ON

And what about her loneliness?
The season's fall/ing in.

Leafy scatterings
across
hedged branchings.

You says,
Talk about yourself. Talk feeling. Talk work.

Clasp, and swirl.
So there is no direction.

Let's begin again.
The catch she is caught in.

You says,
Talk to them. Talk friends. Talk husband.

I must pass. It will pass.
And so what?

You says,
Talk politely. Talk.
Not too fast, not too slow, not too loud, not too low.
Talk-Talk. Gone.

I'd take a word, like loneliness.
And the collected freshness of the world repeats itself.
Thickens. Shoulders up with its etching.
Slithers, long the rib, slips through the tender-minded
utterance.

You says,
Talk.
Keep talking about I don't know what.

And I keep stepping on loosely-skinned words
where dust collects.

The fretted each to each.

THE CALLING[4]

You stepped again into summer's dwelling
waves enduring watering
dusty blue sky.

Dawn's red fireball down-gliding
to bridge-beam with the other shore
hiding abruptly in the binding seam of land/scaping.

With words we look up and out of it.

Language speaks.

Issuing forth
vast stillness.

You, uttering traveller in the twilight's clearing,
resting in the spoken
spit out by your first scream
into the rift of the difference.

AH, AND THE POEM.

Words, a handful of invented surfaces
to scrub themselves down into the tiniest
milli-points of nothingness.

Words, rubbery fences
against voluptuous hoops of sensual steam.

Me, encapsulated by their weightless mass,
consumed and spit out to reinvent my name,
gasping for the new word, the spell, the ultimate,

the task beyond the must or should—
the fearless word which blows through
the dead ends of patterned thoughts,
the worn-out reciprocals,
the stained rooms of hellos and good-byes,
the walked-down stairs of repetitious yes and no's

to give us a chance
to rage with the echo from untied life
where the day, stretched into the world,

spirals through its own vanishing point.

DAY POEMS

This rising day
unlike a worn-out day
crosses swiftly
the stiffening counting
of punctual machinery
and pleads
for a matured duration—

call it Sun/day, Some/day:

this day, in keen play
with the lasting left—

this forced day
coming to be characteristic
neglected and lemon-juice-hot

this day, failing to utter
the—I am/We are—
is going to feed
the orphaned soul
creeping deeply
into bare-skinned chests

to set the blues of
marking love.

This day, like every day,
caught between
the repetition of rise and fall—

this day, unlike yesterday
pours onward—
moody premature spring.

This leaking day
leaps weakly into tomorrow

greening—after all
to let the enfolded possible
exceed.

Counted days, for sure.

My da(y)
ting
says
open eyes
says
touch body be
says
touch finger be tongue
caress touch drive—
dive.

It doesn't say: *work*
says
go and cook
says
feed your day.

Take it
with eyes wide open
and wandering
with
the prevailing unsaid.

Sometimes
I claim for the lasting

a kind
(of)
puffing hope

Sometimes
I worry
(too/and/much) about

my slowly sudden-aging body
the evaporating known

and my little weight on this wallowing earth.

SPRING/ING

This day, after all
this day is peeking
through the misty sun
catching straight forward
last feeble flakes.

This day settles down
with loosening tension
leisurely bending
and suddenly sprouting.

This day branches
out and through—

touch stone fast
touch hot burn slow—

rise
into the weightless dive.

Let's say,
chirping air pre-summer night

penetrating milky green crickets
are out and turning on
the dimmed sky to invisible sparks

I speak of May, where held-back coughing
is audible on the balcony close by
opened dusty windows and screeching doors

I speak of the unbearable joy
to be suddenly exposed—

bright delicate blossoming
dictating nakedness.

Be barefoot,
sweating and heated up
nature's
ongoing undoing

is tricking the ticking.

The moon courting up there
and shivering asleep.

The glistening night
packaging the dry mighty polyphony,
concerted multiplicity.

Cricketing creatures awake.

I talk about the piercing invisible,
the branching coming on to me,
my ride with casual naturing

the pass over—

each to each
amasses,

stirring up my glance.

Making my breathing inspiration
sharpened for entry
to this
portion of time

in the middle of
all the slippages towards me.

Not that I would write about
the welcomed-sooner darkness,
the middle-zoning endless suddenness
where the subtle turns into the drastic.

I try to watch the darkening,
yes I see
not phases, not clear distinctions,
the final is always ahead
catching my sight
like just now.

Rain that is not really raining, not pouring,
drizzling invisibilities,
faintly audible, almost exceeding time in its
creeping streamy dripping.

I see the fully-greened leaves,
bending, in their heightened state.
I see the unpredictable twirling of one leaflet,
a sudden trembling
hit by the tiny mighty drop/ping.

Calendar scattered
in the hollows of my memory.

Dangling in an image.
I am in the pause
to justify the broken phrase,
spinning the lipping around.

A HAND FULL OF HOPE.

An empty sky
on my translucent skin,

soaked dreams
wetting the careless day

blue fading into blue—

days still stand
ripening
into long stretched moments.

My life, picked up by the day
like falling leaves
feeding back their tree.

Every morning
the day pulls out my dreams—
eyes, so wet,
releasing the awakening backwards

eyes, so wet,
still bound to the black mirror
from where underneath begins

eyes, so wet,
merging with the forgetful
transparency of the day.

One morning, when you wake up,
pushed out of the dream of eternal youth
unharmed,

yet with a bunch of scattered hopes
slipping out from your helpless hands—

one morning, when you wake up,
facing your twin's darkened sight,

a new love steps forth
from the hoop of the breathing night,
and you begin to love
this blinded spot
that cannot be saved.

TIME IS A GRANTED LUXURY.

Each morning you wake up
with an eye-opener,
a leap of faith.

Days pass by themselves
hop off swiftly.

You try to stay on time's side—
each hour counts you up and out.

No one leaves this earth alive.

You are walked through
the seamless seasons of your life—

touched skin
well of tears
fist on the laid table.

FOR THE LIVING IS TACITURN

THE DAYS ARE COUNTED IN THEIR UNMEASURABLE PERPETUATION.[5]

Time resides finally
in the name of black stones.

Counting ahead your uncountable steps,
your slightly trembling breath.
Counted is this day's uncountable course.

Time spreads over time, stills, resides,
lays down. Forgets to forget.

Here you go
and go on
in sandy solitude:
the things untouched by words—
you pass them as they pass through you.
Their inspirit leaves no traces.
Sand covers the horrified knowing.
Your uncertainty grows into knotted densities.

Here you go
and go off the time.

Stone, lasting witness.
Water, conqueror of life.

Motion and its shadow.

What is
is folded and folded again.
What is
is flowing and flowing itself.

Here you go
and go through an immensity of self-evident traces
and lost steps.
Here you go
and go through bare-skinned names.
Here you go
through and through
almost arriving.

To be here—
dwell closely in the roofing of the unsayable.
To be here—
spot with your exposed hands the unraveling activity.
To be here—
feel the pulse of permanence.
To be here—
is one time only
and never again;
the fleeting world is you.

Yours is the time of the Sayable.
Speak and bear witness.

Go in sight and sighted.
Kindle what is given to you.

LONGING—

a strong medicine
to stay alive
among
what we never had
and what is forever lost

Longing—
an intangible hand
which unites us sleepwalkers
on the rocky life.

WHAT DO WE DO WITH STRANGE THINGS?

We circle around them
with speech and
we go on a long way

a way that lasts?
a way that never ends?
a way that survives us?

We do not go main stream

we go
we go

on side ways
on rocky roads
on sandy trails
on hidden paths
on adventurous routes

we go
we go

offering ourselves to the quest/ion

we go
we go

over the deaths of our ancestors
bone to bone
in the same earth

When we die
is the tree dying too?

When my tree
is cut

will I become
burning wood

or blank paper

for the next generation?

Am I natural?

TO THE LIVING AND THE DEAD

Life is short,
the days are long.
Human life,
this milli-second invasion
pressed into the geology of rocks
and things.

Me:
air born,
spit out by unlashed soul,
dizzied by uninhabited sight.
Catching breath
at the edge of things.

To live:
a puff,
burning itself out.
Riding on words,
shaking things loose.

To die:
we go and stay
in the rotation of generations.
Pause—
on the tide
that never stops
arriving.

LET'S GO ON

As if there were another voice
at the edge of no return
as flesh goes by.

For now it is a matter
to feel the year swinging wider
as the clock sets the knots lower.

Later,
you will sail
with the vague sweet chanciness
where it will be
as it has become.

Yes, let's go.

AND NOW

You have been here before, haven't you
ascending into the realm of uncreated things

unfinishing
worked-up story all over
anew

tongued by an image.

Seasonless,
there flaming,
the road reaching down.

Forwardness,
here sensuous being,
off/place,
mixing ever-tighter
the wrapped
layers of the real.

LET IT BE SO

She started in
on the names
of the unmarked ones,
someplace daylight
had never been.

She might as well have stayed in the spot
where you cannot be found.

With the sensation of there not being enough,
the question about the place of origin
wafting over the blurry ongoing
and steady perishing.

Love spit it forth—
pulling consoling necessity
up out of the lassitude
of the world's lateness.

Love spit it forth—
the whole story held up,
laid out at once,
doubled.

Suddenly
the others face
the looking,
immersion
into the almost
invisible

taking form.

ONE MORE TIME AND AGAIN

Every now and then
our designation
from a sudden glance
into the passage of
sweet appointment.

Every now and then
our scripting gestures
into the story line.

Every now and then
our little extra bit
trademarking
with the by-pass.

Every now and then
our instant shape
in the appearing
clearing
that breaks with
perfection

to share the day.

ALL RIGHT

In many ways I am growing young.

All right.
There is this fluttering kind of
hope—
remember
a draft of shadowed
onwardness.

I think of milli-second chained details—
twisting my story,
still down on it.

All right.
I turn to the
faceless attention
aiming for the brightest spot,
the only clue I have.

AFTERWARD

Another willed day
stretched into the dark
and the radio
pressed on
with the same bad news.

A thing that happens,
plugged-in reality.

Correct.
We got it right.

And the righteous pleasure
of waiting
to no avail.

Meanwhile
I am preparing supper
between faxes and phones.

Thawing surfaces
regrouping instabilities.

Another willed day
is slipping off.

What is it that leaks?
Where is the track of words?

My slow catch
slithering through.

Mere ongoing being,
resistant to throw into imbalance,
pressed out with definitions—
a willed frame around our scene,
a handful of backboned meaning.

There it is,
the must-pass
goes by and by,
the tip frothing incomplete
and bouquets of instances,
swaying slightly.

When does it change?
Offspring ripples, teases;
my monologue
is
interrupted.

TO DAY

Today is every day
and every day is one less.

A handful of
clicking probabilities
at the hook of
the inevitable.

LIFE'S EMBRACE.[6]

Your embrace glides between yes and no,
calls for what you keep dormant
between the breathing story lines.

We are in the midst of the act of life
shaken and blessed
strong and weakened,
humble and rocked.

What comes and goes
vanishes and rises anew
touching the body of an idea—
lover's eyes closed
the gate opens—

stay lit up like sensuous fireworks.

PART II

POETRY AS AN ACT OF PEACE[7]
AN OUTLOOK FROM THE UNTHINKABLE

We live in a world that is shaken by war and terrorism. The belief in the good and that humans can live peacefully is tested once more. Through TV and other modern media, the whole world has become one body of "judges and executioners." Nobody can live innocently anymore. The scenes in the media merge into one virtual reality.

Especially in times of unforeseen danger, psychologists, philosophers, poets and artists are called upon to take a stand, to throw anchors into the vast sea of bottomless uncertainty.

What role, if any, do poetics and poetry play in such a situation that is saturated with burning issues?

At first glance, this question seems too far-fetched. Poetics, the theory of poetry, simply reflects upon the nature of poetry and the place it had in the past and has in our day. In that sense it has no direct answers, unlike psychology, which (like some religions) offers explanations for human suffering. Poetics is, at best, a neighbor to philosophy, the art of thinking that raises the quite-right questions, hangs in there and elaborates to the fullest. Poetics and poetry love difficult questions, but will not give explanatory answers. They fill the in-between.

Poetry ...weaves and unweaves reflections...
touches the body of an idea...
eyes closed, the words open.[8]

What umbrella were we given
against war
why is Bush not fighting himself
on the battlefield
delegation elevation
frustration
and the world's question
mark

the child cuts the throat of the doll
and wants to know
if Bush will enter the child's kindergarten
if war means war is here all over
and the child paints
the colors of the rainbow
underneath soldiers
and a police force to guarantee
that nobody will be harmed
in this deadly game

and the child doesn't get it
that this God she prays to for forgiveness
that this very God
allows unjustified war.

The child holds hands with her parents
in the marching of four thousand
small colorful human beings
casting the spell
calling
calling
calling
for
peace

the word resurrects
pushed out and up
by waving flags:
peace

for the strong and tender greening
on the rim of difference

we are amidst the other kind and
the mandatory plurality of death

sun is strong burning
in a cosmos of vulnerable skins
sun breaking the light further

(the angels need humans to walk in)

turn on the light

nose up yet deeply into
the greening

and yes it does it does
call me
to embrace my love

Poetry does not excuse. It has neither excuses nor explanations for human shortcomings, weaknesses, unfaithful acts, intolerant behavior and violence. It also is not condemning or moralizing. Its responsibility is to name a thing by its true name,[9] to put a finger on it. This demands a courageous saying that does not use explanations or lies.[10]

Politics easily distorts words, twists their meanings around, strangles them into a straightjacket. A bloody war becomes a "preventive war." "We make a simple intervention" means we go for the war. One does not fight the enemy, one "fights the regime." Murdered civilians are "deceased individuals," enemy soldiers are "flushed in hundreds" like you flush a toilet. These soldiers are not courageous; they are "fanatics" and "zombies" to be eliminated. Yet soldiers killed by their own country's bombs are "under friendly fire." Octavio Paz brings the ambiguous power of words, in everyday language or poetic language, right to the point when he writes:

> ... Words are uncertain
> and speak uncertain things
> But speaking this or that,
>   they speak us.[11]

Poetry helps to distance us from words that speak to us and through us, from poisoned language; it lifts us out from routine linguistic habits.

My previous poem "What umbrella were we given against war" tries to call war by its true name, and asks for "the strong and tender greening." Poetry also surmounts the boundaries of its own language. It is a verbal incantation that provokes a spray of mental images in the reader or hearer. Poetry is heard with the ears but seen only with the mind. The operative mode of poetry is imagining.[12]

Poetry is
...the migrations of millions of verbs, wings and claws, seeds and hands;
the nouns, bony and full of roots, planted on the waves of language;
the love unseen and the love unheard and the love unsaid: the love in
love.[13]

War cannot be thought of without thinking of peace.
The noun "war" migrates and talks of what it is silent about: the love
for the sake of love. In this sense forgiveness, as an outlook around the
unthinkable, is instilled through poetry.

Poetry is merciless yet inclined to forgive: it is merciless in its naming,
yet it forgives by opening up to countless possibilities. It makes the
unthinkable thinkable by breaking the rules. What has been locked up
in reductionistic dead-end discussion gets cracked open in saying the
unsayable: the love in love. Poetry is merciless in its unveiling as it
opens the curtains of our being, yet forgiving by acting as a shelter for
further nudity.[14]

As Pablo Neruda says:

> *Poetry is an act of peace.*
> *Peace goes into the making of a poet as flour goes*
> *into the making of bread.*[15]

— ❦ —

WHAT IS POETRY?

Poetry is an act of peace.

This is of course a strong statement, and I have serious questions that
each poem can live up to this ideal. Yet by more closely encircling the
nature of poetry, we might learn how to knead the dough to become
that bread.

What is poetry? Indeed, this is a vast question. There are so many different poems, countless as grains of sand on the beach. Readers and writers of poetry have contrasting preferences. Despite the different kinds of poetry, we can recognize a poem by the effect it has on us. As Milan Kundera pinpoints, it is characteristic of poetry to let something shine in its beauty:

...poetry casts a cloak woven of most sublime words over our ridiculous clothes. It turns us into kings and queens.[16]

Poetry gives the mundane, the ugly, the struggle, all our shortcomings, and our endless attempts a cloak. The cloak changes its appearance. As it covers, it uncovers. Through the cloak poetry reveals itself in a protected way, so we can see it. This is an act of mercy.

Yet how to make something appear beautiful? Using words like nice, gorgeous, or magnificent doesn't do it. On the contrary, any attempt to beautify ends in a disaster, much like when you use too many colors to paint, you end up with a gray-mouse painting. It becomes as boring and trivial as pornography that shows everything and reveals nothing.

The cloak is woven of most *sublime words*. When and how can we turn words into the *sublime*?
Let me illustrate this with a poem by José-Flore Tappy:

> *The path,*
> *hesitating*
> *like a hungry animal*
> *rubbing between our feet,*
> *flees*
> *and comes again*
> *underfed*
> *it bites at our heels*
> *and leaves us secretly.*[17]

Can you find any outstanding words? We all use these words: path, animal, feet, heels. The poem consists of simple, commonsense words, easy to understand. What is it saying? It talks about the path. I think about our life-path. The path is compared to a hungry, hesitating animal that comes and rubs between our feet, flees, comes again, underfed, bites at our heels and leaves secretly.

The path turns into an animal, yet stays as a path. The path doubles. We see two scenes at play: the literal path and the image or metaphor of the hungry animal. It is a well-known fact that we cannot know our path of life in advance, nor can we determine it. Our reality is renewed through a unique presentation in poetic imagery. This other manner of thinking looks out from the unthinkable.

Poetry multiplies the viewing and leaves one in-sight.

— ❧ —

POETRY—WHAT FOR?

The question *Poetry—what for?* is indeed a quite paradoxical one. It evokes the idea that poetry can be used for a specific purpose. Yet poetry, like any art, opposes direct utilization. Thus, poetry doesn't get worn out like clothes that go out of fashion. Poetry keeps its shape. It's always ready for us, always there.

Let us come back to Neruda's provocative poetic statement and ask ourselves: *How is poetry an act of peace which can instill peace in the making of a poet?* Isn't this in opposition with the notion that poetry is purposeless? Even though poetry is, as such, unproductive, this doesn't mean it is useless. Poetry is serviceable.

Neruda is not saying poetry can be used to make peace. Poetry is not peaceful, nor does it bring peace. Poetry is an *act* of peace. He elaborates on this through thinking his imagery:

> *Peace goes into the making of a poet as flour goes*
> *into the making of bread.*

He is not saying the poet becomes peaceful when writing, not that peace is coming to him. He says peace goes into the making of a poet. We can see two acts in motion: peace goes into the poet that is in the making, and it makes the making of the poet.

An act is an accomplishment, an achievement that has to stand on its own feet. It is a clear step on its own. An act with its clear-cut beginning and end is more framed than *a making* in its process orientation. An act is a performance. What is an act of peace that steps forth in poetry? The writer needs to keep working to find the exact wording until the felt sense of the message is in agreement with the poem. The poet has to endure an inner struggle where words are in competition with each other. Poetry that wants to be precise does not allow bargaining with words, no plea for a compromise. The poet has to go a step further and search for new word-combinations for what is already there.

Therefore:
Poetry is deschooling our way of thinking.
Poetry is useless thinking: the reward is the breakthrough.
It tricks the thought into overcoming itself.

Let me further demonstrate this other manner of thinking with excerpts from the poetry of Jorie Graham. Her poetry holds her poetics: you can never quite get it, and poetry makes you feel good about *not getting it.*[18] Even the title of her newest book of poems, as presented on the dust jacket, puzzles the reader: "Did I hear it right?"

N   E V E *poems* R[19]

The title in spread-out, capital letters lets me read it in many folded
ways through its blank spaces:
— *never* appears as *n ever*, a forever, forevermore
— *poems* is written into the space between the letters E and R of the
title NEVER. I read the title and it throws me off and makes me muse.

Is poetry itself about the "never-ever," and/or is poetry a coming-in-
between? You read two single words and you are taken into a thought-
building with open windows that stretch your imagination.

We live in a highly speedy time. Poetry is even more speedy, yet it
slows you down to dwell between its letter combinations.

Poetry is a light show—
close-ups into the dark and fading.

From Graham's poem "Ebbtide":

> *I am a frequency, current flies through. One has*
> > *to ride*
> > *the spine.*

She speaks of an *I* and dissolves it at the same time: the *I* is a frequency
and current flies through. She goes on to replace the *I* with the *One*. It
follows a proclamation that one has to ride the spine. The fallen-out *I*
finds its way into the spine.

The complexity of the concept of the *I* is rolled up in the poem. In
modern thinking, the me-here-and-the-world-there notion is in
question. In these two poetic sentences, a multitude of new possible

manners of imagining the *I* is in sight.

— *I am a frequency*: who am I anyway? I am one among many others.

— *Current flies through*: the *I* is permeable, translucent; current can fly through.

— *One has to ride the spine*: we would think that it is the spine that holds us up as human beings, yet the spine appears as a persona that has to be ridden like a horse. The words suggest a spine that is horizontal. We are not the carriers of our spines; the spine is carrying us. We have to hold on so we won't fall off.

With this image, she brings the reader to the question: "What is life and death?" As long as we ride the spine, we are in motion, alive. What is left for sure when we are dead are our bones under the earth. We have no control over our bodies; we are just on a ride.

Jorie Graham, at the frontier of a thinking of another kind, loosens the boundaries of our common notions of identity. Her translucent vision of us, as frequencies where current flies through, suggests a humble attitude. This can serve as a harbor for mercy. The current that flies through me is also separate from me.

This suggests to endure …*the rim of difference./We are amidst the other kind and /the mandatory plurality of death.*[20]

Graham's poem ends like this:

> *Done, the birds fly*
> *off. I can see through the trees,*
> *through the cane grove, palm grove, out far enough into*
> *   the clearing where*
> *the spine of the picked-clean story shines.*

II POETRY:
THE OTHER MANNER OF THINKING

THEMES

The following poem talks about the other voice. In contradiction to our so-called "inner voices," the small talk in our heads that accompanies our behavior, the other voice is a distanced, nameless voice.

LEADING IDEA

— Before you write, you listen. In order to get into writing a poem you have to pay attention to the other voice that suddenly may visit, which gives you the material to work on.

— Poetry is not an extension of your inner life; poetry enters you as a directionless move from nowhere to everywhere.

— The poem is not a representation of your emotions and sensations; however, they can be a stirring motivation for your writing.

— You have no ownership over a poem, only a responsibility that it can stand on its own feet. We call this aesthetic responsibility.

— The poem shows that what appears to be "very personal" is simply human; it can happen to everybody.

In writing poetry you first listen and follow the voice
chased by a sudden appearing image.

In writing poetry you attend the voice.
Beyond your stammering,
between your understanding,
the voice hits your mind and
distracts your appetite for boxed order.

In writing poetry you un/cover the voice.
Untouchable, it sets us down in the core of the matter
and leaves a mark to nowhere
in a place that is air born, breath-taking.

Poetry—this distant call,
like a flicker,
a sudden shooting star.

This other voice
has no past with your inner conversation,
has not yet a future with you,
it transits in the speed of light and is hard to catch.

This other voice
doesn't make up for anything
and is gone unless you see it behind closed eyes.
Dreamingly, feet on earth, touchbelly.
Poetry is thinking the unthinkable,
is seeing it before it speaks.
It hits the ground prior to its landing.
It is soil to our soul.
Poetry allows reverie,
the place of twilight,
the embrace of rising darkness
gleaming sun gliding down

at its grip
the unbearable force
of the in-between.

Following *the other voice*, you attend the voice as such, a voice that
has no history with your inner conversations, a voice that you hear
before it speaks, a voice that rides your lingual being anew, air born.
This is an act of peace, a making of a making that, in its timeless sense,
is beyond the need to forgive.

III   WORD KICK-OFFS

THEMES

The following journal entry makes it clear that words have a life
too. Words come and go; new words are invented; others become
old-fashioned or die out.

LEADING IDEA

‒ Poetry aims to touch with its unique use of language. This takes
precise wording, rhythm and quite-right metaphors.

‒ The way we perceive the world is dictated by language. As language
changes, so does our view of the world.

‒ When you write poetry you constantly play with words, endlessly
inventing new combinations and metaphors.

‒ In this sense, you develop a flexibility towards language and how
you perceive the world.

‒ With birth, we are thrown into a given-language world. To grow up
lingual means to re-form mother-tongue, father-voice and society's
anonymous dictate.

‒ Poetry speaks in words that are untouched and fresh. It puts a spell
on the alphabet.

Words have a seasoned life.
Some come and go: fashion words,
like *quality control, trauma, stress, diversity, caretaker, resource*
even though they claim wild, teenage, eternal youth.
They hit the wave, put us out into *brainstorming*. They are battling as
offspring with their parents, putting one foot on the speed, wanting
the ride into opposition, steering the wheel straight forward into a
better future.

There are brand-new words, baby words, yet already breathtaking,
filled with immeasurable information, like *computer, internet,
cel phone.*

Other words get wrinkles, worn-out and sometimes even senile,
mocked, or restricted by the next generations to make way for their
own superpower words: *communism, primal, handicapped, retarded,
Negro.*

Some words are always used and are very old, yet never shrink, keep
ever-alert, like *sun* and *moon, day* and *night.*

Many words are middle-aged, gray, mainstream street walkers, sleepy
morning passengers, or words to go, starters, take-outs to go off into
one's own entertainment: *this is fun, super, this is fucking good,
see you later, what's up, I love you, goodbye, this is great.*
They need a little slap, a wake-up sign, permission to go on, a
handshake, an embrace to connect.

And there are words that keep walking through generations,
almost ghostlike, timeless winged creatures, waving into
our consciousness, always in exodus, yet never dying out:
freedom, peace, war, love, death, art, suffering, healing.

Words stir, words annoy,
words are silenced,
blame, scream, yell, shout,
console, adore, caress,
miss the point and hit pointlessly.

Words are dry and bony,
fleshy and mossy,
melt away on our tongue,
get lost in the other's eye,
disappear into books and reappear,

don't come when we need them,
come too fast or slow down at a crucial moment.

Through words we are endlessly approaching
and this is their destiny, their justification.

IV   IN-MOMENT

THEMES

The following text demonstrates that we cannot live in "the moment."
"The moment" is a mere construct of our minds. In reality there is just the
come-go, the ever-present future and the sunken past.

LEADING IDEA

─ It is a common belief that we can live in the moment if we only pay full
attention to it. Countless promising methods on the therapy market aim to
have a key to the paradise of "being in the moment" despite the fact that
nobody can reach this state.

─ This longing for a timeless immersion, like in a womb, is an anthropo-
logical reality.

─ When you are totally immersed in writing poetry, you forget to think
that you think; there is no boundary. You are in the garden of words.

─ You are in "the catch of eternity," in a dreaming place, fully awake.

─ Poetry and writing poetry can absorb you so much that you forget the
time and you are cradled in the illusion of "being in the moment."

─ It plants the wanting; it stirs our longings; it makes us see the other
shore, the possible, the day when we say night.

─ Poetry is exemplary, a mysterious forerunner that leaves no signs to
follow.

How come we want to be totally in the moment?
Covered by it, absorbed by it,
absolutely eaten up by it
to originate polished, vital
to be spit out into a further moment
a moment that is extended moment—
omnipresence.

Then we can say *here we are, this is it,*
that's exactly what I wanted all my life—
imperative, pure being.

And then, what is then
when the fulfilled moment is achieved
entirely, completely
when there is no other chance left
and the greening is halted?

No other-over-there
to call for, to yearn for.
All over—non-responding,
no grip on my talking mind.

(The back-forward undertaking ceaselessly loosened—
undone, disengaged)

And then, what is then?
I guess: all over
seepage
and an overall
icy
condition.

You come to pass.
And what is that—
moment skips,
hops
like wild rabbits—

your viewing narrows and widens alike
duration, prospect, foresight
like waves breaking over its own breaking
forced continuation for no destination.

Or shouldn't I say,
here there is a narrowing and
here another pressed open.

The perfect moment
continuum—
forgetting has my striving.

V   THE DEPTH OF DEEP

THEME

The following is a discourse about the meaning of "deep" and
elaborates that the depth of "deep" is lost... but where?

LEADING IDEA

— Wanting to write "deep" does not work. Attempting to go "deep"
lifts you up to superficial romanticism and worn-out clichés. When
you dive, you soon come up to catch your breath.

— A poem has "depth" when its word surface is translucent like clear
water, when you keep asking yourself: "Does the text really say what I
think it says?"

— Writing takes *the second look*: you train your imaginary perception.
You go back in your mind to that place and stay there, lift the cover,
open the box. What else is there? At first glance, you see and you do
not see; you notice and it drips away from you like a drop of water.
With the second look you allow yourself to be soaked; you watch it
closely with full attention.

What is depth anyway? In the earlier days, people looked up to
the sky in awe. The deeper meaning came from above, from God.
Deep was *high*. If something went deep it touched from an
unreachable height.

Then humans got high from being deep, deep into their psyche,
deep into the heart or belly, you name it.
And now there is no up nor down
a flimsy everywhere,
horizontal, flat, depth is
neither in something nor out of something,
not even through something or from something else.

Sucked-up dominant final hold,
many-ness vaguely shaped.
Ever-tightness, ceaselessly loosening plan.
The neverlasting moment,
a gate from nowhere to nowhere.
What is next—the fifth dimension?
Audible in-between-ness?

Wound of cracked meaning.

Comprehension gone
before one's looking goes.

Water—the only depth into which we
dive, in order to return alive.

VI   An Outlook at the Surface

Themes

These last two journal entries talk about the changing and the
unchanging, or the changing unchanging. The first scene describes
what comes to the author's mind one morning in spring, drinking tea.
The trigger for the second scene is a phone call with her mother.
Aging changes our bodies, yet the voice usually remains the same.

Leading idea

‐ You start to write by paying attention to the first hint, the first
word or sentence that comes to your mind, and take off with that.
You make a statement and then you have to follow it.

‐ Nature is our teacher. Observe it closely and imagine it. Its
asymmetric beauty touches our sight and loosens our need for a
neat and clear-cut thinking order.

Every morning, almost every morning, when I see the black voluptuous
crow on my neighbors' roof, I think I want to write about birds. These
greasy shining creatures with their sharply curved beaks.
I sit and drink tea. The term *change* comes to my mind. Having to
change becomes almost an obsession. We want to change so badly.
Spring is outdoors, just the beginning of it.
Do I want spring to change? Sprouting *gray* grass and *black*
blossoms? Do I want spring to spit out *brown* leaves?

How soothing to have a mother's voice.

This sentence entered
and makes me think *I have to think about it*
puts me on the spot, and I go blank,
go nowhere with it.

My mother's voice sounds the same over all these years
in its sound and color and pace
bringing the news that is usually predictable
nothing to add and nothing to complain about
I am glad to hear it
to relax into this familiar other voice
I need to hear so that I can hear.

She wouldn't talk about war or terrorism
she would ask me whether I am healthy.
Yes, I am doing fine... and just on the verge of hanging up, I quickly
ask about her health. She is now a widow, over eighty years old, and
steps eternally slow on this earth—her wrinkled hands around a
walking stick, the same stick my father would use.

This unchanged mother-voice acts as a timeless embrace.

Poetry sets the foundation for another manner of thinking.

> *This house of thought has round windows*
> *with an outlook from the unthinkable*
> *that spirals in and out*
> *of resistance.*
> *We might understand*
> *that it overstands our grasping mind.*

Thinking the unthinkable: what cannot be thought out can be seen and form-ulated through a metaphor. Poetry sets a counter-force to daily life language. It reveals what else could be in a deviation of language. It even breaks the rules of grammar and orthography and checks on our thinking.

> *Modern poetry is contrary to rule,*
> *yet it makes sense.*

It challenges our striving for clear-cut answers, like a mockingbird that allures and disappears. We get it and we don't get it. An outlook from the unthinkable is quite a paradoxical position. It suggests an outlook, a viewing that looks out of itself.

If forgiveness has a color, it must be the color of the dove of peace.

ENDNOTES

1. *Crossing Boundaries: Explorations in Therapy and the Arts—A Festschrift for Paolo Knill*, EGS Press 2002, a free translation of the poems in *Tiefe liegt auf der Hand oder von der Kunst am Obergrund zu bleiben* (Depth at the Surface or The Front of Lyrics)

2. Revised, first published in *POIESIS: A Journal of the Arts and Communication, Volume V*. EGS Press 2003

3. First published in *POIESIS: A Journal of the Arts and Communication, Volume V*. EGS Press 2003

4. Revised from *POIESIS: A Journal of the Arts and Communication, Volume II*, EGS Press 2000, p. 80

5. Inspired by Yves Namur, *Die sieben Pforten*; revised from EGS Newsletter 2000

6. Revised from EGS Newsletter 2002

7. See Pablo Neruda in *The Poetry of Peace*. Edited by David Krieger, Capra Press, 2002

8. Octavio Paz, *The Collected Poems of Octavio Paz*. New Directions, 1991, p. 487

9. Thich Nhat Hanh, *Call me by my true names*. Parallax Press, 1999

10. Hilde Domin, *Abel steh auf*. Reclam, 1979

11. Octavio Paz, *The Collected Poems of Octavio Paz*. New Directions, 1991, p. 625

12. Octavio Paz, *The Other Voice: Essays on Modern Poetry*. Harcourt Brace Johanovich, 1990, p. 155

13. Octavio Paz, *The Collected Poems of Octavio Paz*. New Directions, 1991, p. 483

14. ibid, p. 115
15. Pablo Neruda in *The Poetry of Peace*. Edited by David Krieger, Capra Press, 2002
16. See Milan Kundera, *The Book of Laughter and Forgetting*. Harper Perennial Classics, 1994
17. José-Flore Tappy, *Gestampfte Erde*. Edition Howeg, 1988
18. From a radio interview, NPR, USA, January 2003
19. Jorie Graham, *Never: Poems*. Ecco Press, 2002
20. An excerpt from "What umbrella were we given against war," p. 64.

⁓ ACKNOWLEDGEMENTS ⁓

Grateful acknowledgement is made to the staff at EGS Press—editors Shara Claire, Stephen K. Levine and Elizabeth Gordon McKim, and production manager/designer Kristin Briggs—who helped me bring this work into its present form.